Insureomatopeia

Poems by
George Jack

Tilting at Windmills Press, Overland Park, KS

INSUREOMATOPEIA by George Jack
Copyright 2024 by George Jack. All rights reserved.

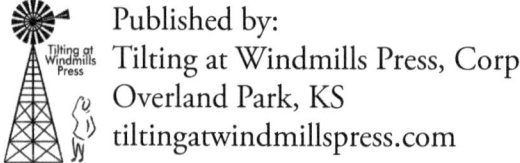
Published by:
Tilting at Windmills Press, Corp.
Overland Park, KS
tiltingatwindmillspress.com

You may not reproduce, modify, copy, distribute, store in a retrieval system transmit, display, publish, sell, or license any information from this document in any form or by any means, electronic, mechanical, photocopying, recording, scanning, or otherwise, without the expressed written consent of the author or copyright holder(s) except for the use of brief quotations for a book review.

ISBN: Print 978-1-7374268-8-2
       E-Book 978-1-7374268-9-9

LCCN: 2024933665

First edition

Printed in the United States of America.

Interior design: Laura Orsini, Panoply Publishing
Photos: Unsplash, AI, Chantal M. Roberts

Dedication

To all fans of Insurance Poetry
who didn't know they were fans yet,
and
To all martial arts fathers and sons,
all Kohai who have lost their Sempei
too soon.

Also by George Jack

Don't Play Catch With Jelly
(with Jennifer Rackley)

Popsicle Insurance

Indiglorious

Contents

Foreword vii

I. Metaphrase and Paraphrase:
   Classic Insurance Poetry Imitations 1

   I Drove Uncovered as I Plowed 2
   Covered Cause of Lossymandias 4
   Fire or Ice 5
   Insurescape With the Fall of Icarus or Ode to a Cretian Burn 6
   Hope Is Not the Thing With Feathers 8
   Shall I Compare Thee to a Policy? 9
   Lovely as a Form CP 10
   O Coverage My Coverage 11
   From Umbrellendemyon 12
   Thirteen Ways of Insuring, or Needing to File
      an Insurance Claim Caused By, a Blackbird 14
   (Uninsu)Red Wheelbarrow 17
   The Coverage Not Taken 18
   Because My Car Could Not Stop For Traffic 19
   In Xanadu Did Work Comp Khan 20
   No Clod Is an Island 22
   Hard Market Day 23
   Parametric Tautogram and EPLIku 24

II. From Miami to Menemsha (Martha's Vineyard)
    New Poems 25

   Miami Heat 26
   Duende 29
   Mortimephesis 29
   Klimtimitation 30
   Watching Oxygen 31
   Contton-Canditopia Candycottontopia Candycottoninuum 32
   Onomateopequod 34
   The Time the Old Man of the Mountain
      Met the Indian Head 36
   Gobbleopolis 40

Lullaby Triolet (for Mom) 41
Softly Evercloaked in Vacuum Voids of Light 42
Nosferatofurkey 45
Fuminfinitum Dans Le Bleu 48
Sanchin 50
Menemsha 54

About the Author 57

Foreword

I'VE NEVER BEFORE been asked to provide a foreword to someone's book; that is until now.

The inimitable George Jack, fearless in his approach to knowledge, writing, and exploring the unexplorable asked, and I consented.

What might have been in George's mind as he formulated this request? Who knows, as I do not know George extremely well, but what I do know of him provides me with a level of respect, circumspection, consideration and awe. For the undertaking of writing a book – any book – requires dedication, fearlessness and might I add a modicum of madness. At least that is what I think.

George is a rare commodity and one which (or who) should be savored. He is a fount of knowledge; some obscure, some insurance related, some driven by a love of music and the sublime, some just downright based in minutiae. Yet, all of it seems so timely and on point when he utilizes it.

This, his book of poetry, reflects all of the foregoing.

George reminds me of what used to be termed as a "renaissance man." No, not the Danny DeVito character from the movie of the same name – although I am pretty certain that George appreciates this reference. I mean the classical use of this term meaning one who has many talents and areas of learning and knowledge. That, to me, is an almost perfect moniker for George.

So, please enjoy what he has written.

You may find it amusing, thought provoking, silly, obscure, or some other descriptor that best fits for you. I'll suggest to you that George will be less concerned with what you think and more appreciative of your taking the time to read his works.

Good reading.

Casey Roberts
February 2024

I.

Metaphrase and Paraphrase: Classic Insurance Poetry Imitations

I Drove Uncovered as I Plowed

I drove uncovered, as I plowed
Uncovered, plowing snowed driveways
Uncovered by a policy
Not by an auto policy
So I could save some currency
To buy my love some daffodils.

When all at once I saw a crowd
Pointing at my truck, and plow
In finger pointing unison
I then realized I slid on ice
Off of the road, beside the lake
Hoping that I would not crash
Also no triple AAA, beneath the trees.
Charging trees, like a light brigade
Trees stretched, a never ending line
Til finally, I hit, plow first
A tree, smashing snowstormedly
With force that would have made Joyce cry
Joyce Kilmer, not my love named Joyce.

I hoped insurance agents would
Forget I had no policy
And with their jocund company
Spare me my uninsured expense.
But now, on my couch I oft lie,
My Joyceless couch, for she left me,
For a risk manager who buys
Joyce all the daffodils she wants

As my heart with loneliness fills,
Languishing lonely as a cloud.

I Wandered Lonely as a Cloud
William Wordsworth

George Jack

Covered Cause of Lossymandias

I met a traveler from a land of antique insurance
Not someone who worked for a company with a similar name
He did stand in a claimless desert with antiques near him on the sand.
Half sand sunk, a crashed semi lies, whose front tires
Engine, cab, lay as if in water, grain submerged
But not the sculptures, hutches, couches on which books were read,
The hands that made them, not there and long dead,
Then without being asked, the traveler volunteered:
My name is Covered Cause of Lossymandias, Insurance-Less King
Look on these wares, you owners, and despair.
You didn't give a bill of sale, or inventory list
And left in haste not getting trucking risk,
All uninsured, all, scattered 'round this colossal wreck,
The level sands were deeper than I thought,
Antique delivery made not today
Antique and truck sinks, lone sands stretch far away.

Ozymandias
Percy Bysshe Shelley

Fire or Ice

Some say the restaurant I own will end in fire,
Some say in ice.
There's part of me that isn't thinking twice;
I hope my restaurant is done in by ice.
Except, unlike fire, more lethal and warm,
I can't get ice covered as a peril
As part of the Broad causes of loss form.
But if somebody asked me twice
I'd still pick ice
I think I know enough of thaws
That someday the ice would melt away
And I back making cornbread and sweet slaws
For those who've tasted BBQ's desire,
So, as my grill gives my sole semblance of pyre,
CP 10 20's praises I won't tire,
As I sing covered from dreams ending fire.

Fire and Ice
Robert Frost

George Jack

Insurescape With the Fall of Icarus or Ode to a Cretian Burn

According to de Hory
When Icarus fell
No one knew what the peril would be.

A farmer was ploughing his field
And had not insured his farm
Against falling objects.

Icarus fell on his barn
And the farmer slipped
On wax

Shooting out from
The edges of
Icarus wings
The farmer slipped
On the wax
And since

His wife owned the farm
He opened Unsignificantly
A work comp claim

She, also Safety Compliance Officer
Laughed, as a claim filed at the edge
Of a forest is as dismissible as

What was left of Icarus
Just enough for Daedelus to fit into
A Cretian urn.

Insureomatopeia

Landscape With the Fall of Icarus
William Carlos Williams

George Jack

Hope Is Not the Thing With Feathers

Hope is the thing with feathers, that I hope
While perched on my soul's shoulder
Doesn't fly off and attack me by say,
Swooping down and tearing a tendon,
Then while I can't move
Flies up to a branch and sings the tune without words
And never stops at all.
Before the Gale from the storm
Abashes the little bird,
I need to know if it has an owner
That has homeowners or renters insurance
So I may file a claim and will ask more
Than a crumb
Of them.

Hope Is the Thing With Feathers
Emily Dickinson

InsureomaTopeia

Shall I Compare Thee to a Policy?

Shall I compare thee to a policy?
Thou wouldst cover me less in accidents.
Though compared to insurance you're lovely
I love my coverage more, in my defense.
When rough winds shake the darling buds of may
And my tree falls into my neighbor's yard,
Though you're beautiful like a summer's day
Tis you I would unflinchingly discard
In favor of a defense for their claim.
Though I have oft admired you from afar
Big picture, I don't want to know your name
Unless you're an insurance agent, too,
Then no insurance would compare to you.

Shall I Compare Thee to a Summer's Day?
William Shakespeare

Lovely as a Form CP

I think that I shall never see
A form as lovely as CP.

A form, for when by perils pressed
I have insurance needs addressed.

A tree that looks at God all day
May also, earthward, fall my way

A tree that may in Summer, bear
Not just birds but a slew of cares

When it topples and then does fall
On my business in the strip mall.

Business begun by fools like me,
May rely on the form CP.

Trees
Joyce Kilmer

Insureomatopeia

O Coverage! My Coverage!

O Coverage! My Coverage!
Our trip is done at last
And happily we had insurance on our watercraft
Beyond belief, we hit a reef, we thought the water deeper
We swerved to miss a tiki boat, their captain was a sleeper
But O, crack, crack, crack
Our hull a wreck, expensive,
Thankful our agency sold us
Coverage Comprehensive.
O Coverage, My Coverage,
Our trip was marred by swells,
The swelling of the wake from waves, towards disaster propelled
Though to have to pay for coverage was not something we desired
At 25 MPH we had the horsepower required.
Now it's back, back, back,
To the state our boat was in,
Our agent thought to include
An exclusion for chagrin.

O Captain! My Captain!
Walt Whitman

From Umbrellendemyon

Umbrella coverage can be a joy forever,
Beyond auto, homeowners, it will never
Forsake you when policy limits hit,
Nor neglect you when negligence's writ
Comes to you in the form of a lawsuit; and
A plaintiff is litigiously acute.
Umbrella coverage will never let you
Pass into nothingness, when lawsuits sting
And you are made to bear outrageous slings
And arrows brought on by a certain claim,
Shame, shame, the courts will all soon know your name.
Therefore, not on any morrow are we wreathing
Flowery personal liability hands to bind us to the earth,
Though rates may raise, for $100 a month,
Up to one million in coverage moves away the pall from
  our dark spirits.

Therefore tis with full happiness that I trace the story
Of Umbrellendemyon. The very music of the name
Is the song of protection against my dog
Causing injury to others, if a guest in your home falls
It will be as if they fell on a bower of musk-rose blooms
When guests are injured staying in your rooms.
At once, adventuresome I send my herald thought
Into a wilderness of potential insurance claims
The rose of insurance coverage never smelled as sweet
By any other name.

Endymion
John Keats

George Jack

Thirteen Ways of Insuring, or Needing to File an Insurance Claim Caused by, a Blackbird

I
Among 20 people on the overcast beach
The only moving thing
Was a blackbird riding a drone

II
I was thinking of the HO3
Wondering why it didn't cover
A falling tree with three blackbirds.

III
Driven mad by his lack of capacity,
The underwriter donned a cape from a Halloween store
And whirled around in circles,
An autumn winded, craze-fueled pantomime.

IV
A man and a woman
And a blackbird
Flying into a moving car's windshield
Are an accident.

V
I do not know which to prefer,
The coefficient of coinsurance or
The codependence of reinsurance.
Convincing the blackbird to insure me,
For the higher deductible.

Insureomatopeia

VI
Garage stalactite icicle javelins pierced my window
Like black-artisanal thickened hyperbaric glass
The shadow of the blackbird
Flying, cawing back and forth
Mocks my declaration page with
An indecipherably high deductible.

VII
O thin men of Hartford and Harvard
You imagined this man as a flock of golden birds
He who so nuancedly rendered blackbird verse
Insurance premium and prosody dazzled the transoms
Of the women around him

VIII
I know accents that make lesser words noble
And lucidly, never piloted an unmanned vehicle
Because I know too, there are no endorsements
For blackbird related perils,
That's what I know.

IX
When the blackbird flew out of my sight,
I heard it soar beyond the fencing,
Uncovered by the farm insurance liability policy.

X
At the sight of blackbirds
Flying next to and covering a green light,
The bawds of the declaration page
Do cry out sharply.

XI
Driving to Connecticut on Route 84
Trucks kicking rocks against his glass
A rock cracked it
He never mistook
The missile flying at is windshield at the speed of his deductible
For a blackbird egg

XII
The river is moving.
The blackbirds must be plotting to swoop down
And pierce my white water raft while I negotiate
A class 5 rapid.

XIII
They scheduled dusk during morning that day
It should have been snowing
But never did
The blackbirds wheeled in the sky
Deflecting inclemencies
The day was austere, postcard perfect, and claims free.

Thirteen Ways of Looking At A Blackbird
Wallace Stevens

InsureomaTopeia

(Uninsu)red Wheelbarrow

So much depends
upon
A red wheel
barrow
We can't afford to
have fall apart,
Unable to be
covered
As a cause
of loss
On the
FP 00 10.

The Red Wheelbarrrow
Willam Carlos Williams

George Jack

The Coverage Not Taken

When roads diverge in a yellow wood
Unlike other kinds of woods, brown, green,
Loss Damage Waivers do cease to be good
Like, if something should fall and dent your hood
Insurance cannot help or intervene.

My car rental agent did think it quite strange
When in renting my car I did arrange
Coverage which the agent did find good
Except for the part that I did pass on
Which left me uncovered if something happened
To my rental deep in a yellow wood.
Before where roads diverged, what could I do?
Trapped in my rented Buick Rendezvous
Regretting not that I was but one traveler
But that, towards yellow woods I would feel fear
In case something happened while driving here.

I will not tell this to the rental guy
Not now, or ages and ages hence,
A tree grows through my Buick Rendezvous
Because I took a third road untraveled by,
Just sitting here, lack of coverage and fear
LDW would have made all the difference.

The Road Not Taken
Robert Frost

Insureomatopeia

Because My Car Could Not Stop for Traffic

Because my car could not stop for
Traffic that kindly stopped for me
The car held only just us two,
The brakes gave out on we.

                      I quickly drove, and knew much haste
                          Into town for a movie date,
                  The previews my wife could not miss,
                          I dared not make us late.

I was distracted by snack thoughts
Of popcorn and sweet Raisinets,
I thought not of a car recall
The manufacturer had sent
About the brakes, my model, make
Needing back to the dealer bring
And maintenance reminders that
I filed among forgotten things.

                      Reminded was I quickly with
                        Adrenaline and precision
                    My movie night was stunted by
                        An Unforeseen car collision

So grateful coverage was spelled out
Upon my declaration page
Since then we stream movies at home
Per my wife, beautiful and sage.

Because I Could Not Stop for Death
Emily Dickinson

George Jack

In Xanadu Did Work Comp Khan

In Xanadu did work comp Khan
Start him a widget factory,
On the banks of the river Alph
Renovating a pleasure dome
Near forests ancient as the hills.

In walls and towers girdled round
He set up his assembly lines
Intending he to mass produce
His Kublai Khan-brand honey dew
And bottled milk of paradise.
But it was not all incense bearing trees, and
Sunny spots of sinuous greenery.
The workforce? Not all dulcimer damsels,
He hired the locals he had to cull from,
Savage skilled labor from
    A Savage Place,
His HR Manager, a woman
    waiting for her
Demon Lover, haunting her
    beneath a waning moon.

In caves of Ice, if workers slipped, did fall,
Or near a fountain, hit by dancing rocks,
Ancestral voices filing work comp claims,
Kublai's business, his refit pleasure dome,
As stately as his pleasure dome it was,
Khan's Dew was operating in a State
Where work comp was the law, and he complied.

And all who heard, they could read on the wall
Big posters they of workplace safety told
Of guidelines, legal statutes follow-ed
No work comp claims? Sales of Khan's Dew were gold.
So please don't close your eyes with holy dread,
Or you might have an accident instead,
No slips, no falls, the accidents were gone,
In stately factory of Work Comp Khan.

Kubla Khan
Samuel Taylor Coleridge

No Clod Is an Island

No agent can insure an island
Entire of itself
Nor may they insure large pieces of a continent;
Those policies don't exist.
If a clod be washed away by the sea,
The policy would not be the less,
Also no one says clod anymore,
A lump of earth or clay.
Any man's death would diminish me
If I owned an island and they were washed away
While napping on a clod from an island I owned
Because I would have no insurance, I know
After a broker told me
No agent can insure an island.
If a bell on top of a clod that was being washed away
Began to toll for me, no one would hear it
So I would be all set, after all set, after all.

No Man Is an Island
John Donne

Hard Market Day

Insureomatopeia

White glittering sunlight bakes the Florida
    hard market
Spotted and sprigged with increases in prices
Realtor's bartering booths cannot get rid
    of products it can't sell
Less homes are available. The morning air
Smells sweet and sour with the lingering
    threat of hurricanes,
A wicker basket gapes and overflows with
    the contents of a
Tropical storm disaster kit. The market glows
With the disbelief of non-renewal notices and
Increased premiums, and clatters with complaints
Like New Englanders forced to wait in bank lines
Three deep, when there used to be bank lines.
At the edge of the market, a wide, arched doorway
    opens,
Pealing an organ playing ballads and devotionals,
Singing of Personal Insurance
    Comprehensive reviews,
The Hard Market uniting policyholders
    in vibrant harmony.

Market Day
Amy Lowell

Parametric Tautogram and EPLIku
(the almost perfect workplace toolkit haiku)

Parametric Perils Pack Profound Problems
Producers Prescribe Policies Per Professionals' Permission
Picturesque Pristine, Pre-Seismic Panorama,
Parsimoniousness Precludes Potential Positivity.

Employee hiring
Equity Made Possible
With EPLI

Original Insurance Poem
George Jack

II.

From Miami to Menemsha (Martha's Vineyard) New Poems

George Jack

Miami Heat

I always thought that was a dumb name
For a professional basketball team
Then I went down there for a week
The week after the hottest temperatures
recorded on Earth
The people in New England complaining
About 80 degree heat
Like the third person back waiting in a bank line
When there used to be bank lines
"This bank line is really long, hah,
must be breakin someone in"
Drop them in Miami for a week
Sure, there is the beauty of the hotel
lights reflecting
Off of the bay near Brickell Key,
undulating like a
Violet cod run, by night,
By day, the ocean water, simmering
hottubidratiously,
Bleaches the coral reefs,
The owner of Mofongo, the only
Puerto Rican restaurant
In Little Havana, prepares
for an onslaught by
Heat strokenagitated zombies,
while rationalizing his

Insureomatopeia

Kids menu to tourists, dumbed down
by mac and cheese
And chicken tenders, the kids stare at their helping of
Pechanga a la Parrilla para niños
As the owner reassures
"Every children loves chicken bresss".
Instead of kinds menu style coloring books,
The Owner contemplates sending tourist children,
Waiting for their food, to go out and color
On his rival's restaurant walls, while the
Heat, so hot, Gunga Din would have given up,
Lawrence of Arabia would never have taken the
Guns at Aqaba, the Florida man
would not have needed to
Tie a generator to the top of his corer-dented
Chrysler town and country or a dodge caravan
and plug in, who he loves more
than his wife at this point,
An air conditioner, not in his window,
but riding alongside him,
He listens to NPR, scientists have
discovered a new state of
Phase change, now in addition
to solid, gas, liquid, there is
Hot. Miami Hot. Miami Heat.
I get it now.

    George Jack

Duende

It is the width of flavor, the space the
    taste of a cocktail takes
In a mouth newly invisipollocked by
    the art of expert mixologicality,
Diminischendo of tension, Blackstock
    and Webbers lightly tapping
To the sound of waves created in the wake
    of a fleet of tiki boats
Lapping, lapis elastilazarus, the blue
    of the evenings lapis lazuli
Wraps around me, lazarusticana, duende
    awakens and I close my eyes
Listening to nylon strings tuned
    to the key of the breeze,
Strophic, repeating, collar button
    loosened
Flutes filled by the siren song of
    sparkling wine
Welcoming me once again
    to the pleasure drone.

George Jack

Insureomatopeia

Mortimephesis

Antipotheosis
Struggles of the butterfly
Who cannot fight the impulse to
Reinhabit their discarded chrysalises
Are voiced in a crescendo of mute cocoonphony,
Painted ladies withdraw curtains,
Monarchs retract wings, heeding this
Unprecedented clarion pulse,
The forest, once lepidopterritorial
Is now a museum of regression and abbreviation
Whose primary exhibit is a
Pageantry of proto-pupa, antithetimorphosis,
Mortamephesis, back to the chrysalis.

George Jack

Klimtimitation

When the Lady With A Fan walks by
The Flowery Garden
You'll wish you had been the one
    to show her
The blossom pallet captured
    by the master's eye,
Romance inducing and vegepiphinatious
    sense-delight,
Nourished by the pure waters
    surrounding the
Island in the Attersee.
One may almost reach in and tug at the
Birch back seeming to peel off
    of the trees in his
Birch Forest near the Beech Grove I.
According to one of his
    Beethoven Friezes,
The Longing for Happiness
Finds Repose in Poetry;
The poets find new expressive
    heights to scale
When marveling at his
Blumengartenmanjaro,
While we aspire to create images
    inducing in our audience
The expression on the face
    of the woman
Cloaked in the olifactileidoscope
    of Klimt's
The Kiss.

George Jack

Insureomatopeia

Watching Oxygen

Lying in the grass, head propped up
Resting on hand clasped, interdigitated fingers
Resplendent in the ethered-leisure of my
Relaxed and country-gentlemancy,

Light is refracted across my vantage point
Through the garlickly-glazed,
Prismystically thin wingspan of the dragonflies,
Every slight movement of their
Stainglassedly slight, thinfinetisimally fanned
Nano-defiant outstretchedness.

The convention which states it is
Scientifically impossible for oxygen to fly
Gives way to a more pleasant
Hypothepostulation
As I relish these moments in which
I have taken this time for
Watching oxygen and sunlight
Dancecandescantly play
   on the arc of their own
Fanfareodynamicality.

George Jack

George Jack

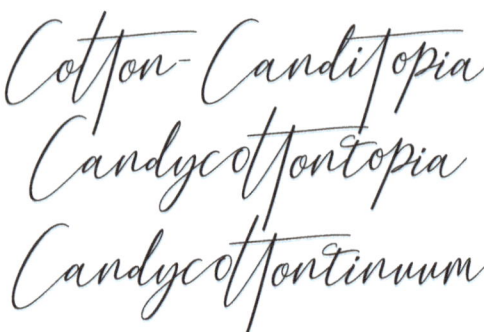
Cotton-Canditopia
Candycottontopia
Candycottontinuum

There's nothing not to love about
A carnival, a festival, a fair.
Something for every amusementality and memory-sense
A candy cottontinuum of fun.

Hurry! Hurry! Hurry! Step right up –
But take your time, enjoy the sights,
The flavors, sounds, the memories in the making;
Smaller hands, clutching tickets
As they wait to thrill again or for the first time,
To the inventively-tentacled and
Multicolored, mirrorluminated rides as they glow by.

Insureomatopeia

There is no food like fair food, carnival food,
Fried dough, sugar-stubbled sweetbreads,
Food of the paradise that is this candy-cotton tops.
Corn dogs, unsewered battered-bastions of bedevildrie and
Fairground flavors, Funnel cakes,
Melting in the mouth at the speed of a carousel,
The song of the merry go round
Calli peacefully cascading through the hearing distance
Like the circle-steady Ferris wheel,
Millionwatted, girder-jangled gear
In the clock of the carney-cathedral
Where we wander to and make our way each year.
The fortune teller, gypsy-girded glass confin-ed all-knowing nomad,
Passes cards offering your randomly shuffled fate, but
Doesn't offer much, her delicious omnipotent grin
Says it all –
You'll be back again next year to see me,
There's nothing not to love about a fair

George Jack

George Jack

Onomateopequod

Narrator, call him Ishmael, he's Ishing, he's dishing
His job is to hunt whales with super swim swishing.
Queequeg is his friend, a goon with big harpoon,
With spears that whoosh he'll kill 10 whales before noon.
They got jobs on the first whaling boat they could grab
That was run by a grim weirdo, Captain Ahab.
When the sea's calm, you'll hear Ahab's smile creaking down,
Like he once was the Mayor of New FrownyTown.
His smile sagging, wooden leg knocking and dragging
With a knock and a zchishchhhh,
   with a knock and a zchishchhhhh……
They whale hunted for Ahab, but never asked he
Why his one leg was people, and one carved from a tree
Then he gathered the crew and he told them the tale
Of how his leg was taken by a great white whale.
Taken…where? Did he hide it under his huge bed,
Or did he, with whale chomping,
   munch-munch it instead?

Insureomatopeia

Ahab showed a gold coin, and he told the crew how
The one who saw a white whale with a wrinkled brow
The first crewman who did, he would make him rich quick
For the whale Ahab looked for was old Moby Dick.
They searched the sea, at the boat's sides waves lap-lapping
Till a yell – Thar she blows! – That meant whale stuff was happening.
Then a great, giantotious whale, made all say WOW!
He was sighted off aft, port, and the starboard bow!
Flooshing water quite angrily out his blow hole,
It was old Moby Dick, mad and out of control!
With a smash! – and a crash! – he ramrodded their boat
Till it sunk, no crew left, only Ish stayed afloat
For a day, night, and day, till his timely rescue
    By a ship, plappy-splashing on the briny blue.
        What we've learned? A harpoon the size of New
        Brunswick
            Needs to be brought along when one
            hunts Moby Dick.

George Jack

George Jack

The Time the Old Man of the Mountain Met the Indian Head

I
NH fables aren't folk tales where giants tend to tread
With the exception of this one, before not heard or read,
How do I know…? It wouldn't be a secret, if I said –
I hope you find this story fun,
Of two that weigh dozens of tons,
It's two or three tall tales in one –
The time the Old Man of the Mountain met the Indian Head.

II
Our story starts way back in time, northwest of South Barnstead,
Where lived an Abenaki tribe near hills, granite, rugged,
Native Americans just trying to keep their people fed,
The rocky soil made it hard for food to grow,
Their Chief sent the call out for one who would know
How plenty back to the ground could be bestowed –
The time the Old Man of the Mountain met the Indian Head.

III
A medicine man used the powers for which he was bred,
He let his mystical senses guide him, till he was led
To a tall granite mountain also serving as a bed
That did sustain the hibernation
Rockquilt-suspended animation
Of he now stirred by incantation –
The time the Old Man of the Mountain met the Indian Head.

IV

Rocks, trees, dirt from the mountainsides displaced, and in their stead
Stood a tremendous warrior, size and strength unbounded
The body of a huge statue, with a great Chief-Like Head
They said people are starving, no food grows at all
Then he clapped his huge hands in response to the call –
And before long the sweetest of raindrops did fall,
The time the Old Man of the Mountain met the Indian Head.

V

Before their eyes there seemed that grew crops to be harvested
While to so many he brought joy, in others he, instead,
With his great size those far off saw him and were filled with dread
So the farmers and townspeople from low and high
Loving to Live Free and not wanting to Die
To deliver them from this behemoth they cried,
The time the Old Man of the Mountain met the Indian Head.

VI

So many wished for the colossus to be contested,
Another granite Goliath woke, all were astounded
He looked much like a massive…Old Man…solemn and bearded
Brushing dirt off his gigantic mountain man clothes
He saw the fellow giant that that he thought did pose
A threat to the people; his fists they then rose,
The time the Old Man of the Mountain met the Indian Head.

VII

Then, towards the Indian leviathan the Old Man sped,
Grabbed him, and then threw him up near where the Moon orbited,
Right after which back towards the White Mountains he plummeted
Settlers, Abenaki alike could just watch
As the crater he made, landing with a Ker-Splotch
Made what today is known as Franconia Notch,
The time the Old Man of the Mountain met the Indian Head.

Insurcomatopeia

VIII
The Indian Head rose, unscathed, completely unwounded,
And with a chop, the Old Man's surprise was interrupted,
As he flew and a gorge-sized hole was made, ground indented,
The giant thought he had sealed the Old Man's doom,
But he rose from what was supposed to be his tomb,
And then water rushed in, making what's now, the Flume,
The time the Old Man of the Mountain met the Indian Head.

IX
What are true miles seemed feet to these gargantuan kindred,
Then they locked arms, each other's demise what they intended
Then they fell, dirt, rocks, trees flew, and the whole state shook, jolted
On the Richter scale it measured more than Thirteen
And the Shakers still Shake from the jumbo crash scene
Which carved out what we know as Tuckerman's Ravine,
The time the Old Man of the Mountain met the Indian Head.

X
The Old Man was the first to rise, then looked out, regarded,
The Abenaki, saw their crops, how they celebrated,
And realized no harm was meant. So, now, educated,
He held out his hand to his up-till-now foe,
And the Indian, he let his gratitude show,
Was helped up, and their separate ways they did go –
The time the Old Man of the Mountain met the Indian Head.

XI
They each gathered a mountain around them, their fight ended,
Now sleep till by those in the six-oh-three they are needed.
The Old Man's face, by weather, time, has since dissipated –
But now? You know a story not told before,
I sure hope it gets retold, then told some more
Of when mountainous of men tried to settle a score –
The time the Old Man of the Mountain met the Indian Head.

George Jack

Gobbleopolis

September's color change and chill
Ushers in, along with leaf peeping
Morning visits from packs of nomadic,
Chandelier-chinned cousins of the grouse;
Covering the outdoor ground in a cloud-gathering of
Wispily-wickered, zebra-feathered wanderers,
An accumulonimbus of aimlessness.
A city whose only denizens are stunted,
Scavenger-peacocks, Their
Body language is all punctuation,
Commas, back-and-forward slashes,
Stutter-struttedly pantomiming
The kabuki-theatri-redundancy of
Their backyard picking ritual
As they methodically,
Straightlinedly, and
Butterballistically
Amble towards nutrition
With all of the en-herkijerkment of
A scarecrow with a skeleton of two by fours,
Arthritically macarenaring
Towards staving off its own, personal
Wintrevitability.

George Jack

Insureomatopeia

Lullabye Triolet (for Mom)

It is not me that's singing at night to my child
It is my mother's voice and she's singing through me
All her best silly songs and her lullabies mild
It is not me that's singing at night to my child.
If at all by the music my baby's beguiled,
It's that my mother's there, singing to her, to me,
It is not me singing at night to my child
It is my mother's voice, and she's singing through me.

George Jack

Softly Everclocked in Vacuum Voids of Light

There is a type of forest goer,
Whose AMC Mountain Guide
Is written on the trees themselves,
Wilderness catalogued in organically-configured fonts,
Individually, Exo-skeletously,
Unfurled over the body of each tree,
Embossed in the corrugations of their own typefaces,
Vegetative monoliths
Deoxyribonucleistically accented
Each benign, bark laden signpost, touch and feel totem poles
Feed their secret signals to the hikers that walk and wander,
Following darkest horizons;
The trees become vertical lines of demarcation,

Their uniquely dioramic loops and whorls
Epidermistically hewn on them,
From within them, like so much
Unintentional and randomly carved Braille.

Which olifactory – sight, or touch,
Turns out the peeping practitioner whose style
Brings one the closest to the beauty
That nature really and truly holds for all?
Ask the young woman, who,
As she grew more ill,
Became practiced in the
Protractional avocation of dying,
Preferring the dimmer visaged caress
On her husband's warm, bald head
To the real thing –

Watching the lukewarm shimmer of
The late summer/early autumn Sunsets
They could no longer,
By sight's constraint,
Share together.

Nature has both an aversion to, and affectation for,
Vacuums.
In the case of so many considered optically irreceptive,
Sightlessness gives way to let in equal parts
Ubersensory awareness and
Will-reinforcing pride.
"Spare us your sighted platitudes, your
Indifferently offered incandescentries –
Light travels too fast for us, anyway."
The delumination of nature lends itself to
All sorts of mysticisms, possibilities.
A leaf may be made, by the blind, to be any color;
Those who peep with sight are stuck
With what color the leaf really is.
A picture is worth only so many words,
The texture of each tree a Rosetta Stone
Whose Beauty and story are restless for caress –
The breezier the forest, the more conversant.
The denser the glade and clearing with sounds
Upon scents
Upon sounds, tangensations,
Bouquets that recommend themselves sweetly and
Nimbly to gentle scent memory, ear,
The more long winded the discourse with the imagination.
Besides, the sighted peep must cease at sunset
With hopes of resuming in the morning –
Whereas, there is a nature lover whose sweet talk and
Acute, touch thirsty caresses
May last all of every hour that is bright,
Every hour is light
When absorbing arts' offerings
On a lifescape softly evercloaked in vacuum-voids of light.

Nosferatofurkey

Insurcomatopeia

Places exist where legend and reality are murky
Such creatures dwell there that might make thy sanity desert thee
But since November's here I thought it prudent to alert ye
That though great meals are what for Thanksgiving we hail
It's a holiday with its share of scary tales
Like this story, with which your ears I shall assail –
The tale of the NOSFERATOFURKEY.

It started way back when the Pilgrims – landed here firstly
And they prepared the first Thanksgiving for Chief Massasurkey
From then til now, the death toll's made surviving turkeys thirsty
Their thirst for revenge, longing to stem the tide
Of the annual slaughter/gobbler genocide
In this dark hour, Butterball black arts were plied –
Towards the summoning of the NOSFERATOFURKEY.

To counter this dire threat affecting them most disconcertly,
A vegetarian voodoo priest was found in Albequerque
Whom, legend said, slew Frank Perdue in ways secret and curstly
Since revenge against man was to what they aspired
He told of a beast that would meet their desires

George Jack

Part ground-fowl, part golem, and one-third vampire –
The dreaded NOSFERATOFURKEY.

(First,) Procure an ounce of blood from Rachel Ray, annoying, perky,
Mix giblets with tofu dyed red by coloring from Durkee,
Then, bring all to the darkest glade of swamp Okee-Finurkee
The turkeys, they did as they were bade,
Gobbled forbidden chants over what they had made
When, from out of the most brackish bog in the glade
Rose the dark-meated death bringer, NOSFERATOFURKEY.

Insureomatopeia

The creature looked like them except much larger, darker, lurky,
With a lust for human blood that when left unquenched, made him irky
But to whomever work it, ever faithfully twould serve he
So it, like an angel avenging, earthbound
On those in charge of every turkey farm found

Took its vengeance, and that night the hills did resound
With the blood-gargled gobble of the NOSFERATOFURKEY.

Next time it comes around, this 4 day freedom fest from worky
And you selfishly gourmet-gorge into some poor, baked, ex-turkey,
Before you take this tale and disregard it as malurkey,
Remember, as you take each gravy-soaked bite
Please, try not to enjoy it too much, or you might
Meet with fowl vindication in your dreams tonight-
From the beak-ed, arch-terrible, NOSFERATOFURKEY.

George Jack

Fuminfinitum Dans Le Bleu

Cigar tips glisten dignifiantly
From the without of a vast, cool indiglue
At a dinner party hosted by the Illuminati
MC Escher manipulates stars and sections of sky
To chords rendered by Picasso's Old Guitarist
Nylon strings vibrating forth Villa-Lobos, Rodrigo, Sor, Torroba,
Keeping timelessness along with tonight's
Masterwork of constellationistic flow.

Afterward, the company retires to the salon for brandy and cigars,
Two rooms over and one floor from
Treasures stores, held in Heaven's high humidor.

Insureomatopeia

For myself, gazing relaxedly from my porchward perspectivity
Dusk ushers in the soup course, and around me
Trees unselfconsciously dispense with their stoic veneer
Posing like hyberbarically held Japanese Kanji

I am privy to moments of imaginationally tethered mysticality
As leaves and branches fan and ripple, silently approbational
In a breeze blown show of one-handed applause –
Mutely offered appreciation of this firmamentous delicacy,
Leeks and onions perfectly golden brown, limber,
Tense, tender ingredients winking out
From a depthless, muddled, bruise-blue vischyssois.

Dispensing with spoon, I pluck from the gourmet borealique
A garlic steeped and ideally enbuttered crouton,
Touch tongue to corner, and
On the edge of the ebb of the forestral ovation
I offer a humble, meager Om –
"In croy-a-ble'"
As I whisper noir et bleu shaded nothings
Into the ear of Gaia herself.

Candles permeate and perfume the curtains of
Mother Earth's boudoir
I feed her croutons a la mode,
Sheep's milk cheese in a peppercorn reduction, I
Improvising the beginnings of haiku, tanka,
"Desire and caress",
"Fingertips, contours,"
"Interpersonal",
We puff Partagas, heedless of embargo,
I open a Cabernet Franc, and as it breathes
I kiss her knuckles, turn her hands over, attend her wrists
Begin reciting our epic to her, as never-to-be-resolved and fathomful
As the blue, the achingly currentless riverblue,
In which the irises of my foreverlover's eyes
Simmer quiescently and are as softly steeped.

George Jack

Sanchin
To Sempei from Kohai

I.
BODY

Tonight is my first class, first lesson, and my feet are cold,
But as the dawn of every first day warms into morning,
I soon forget the unfamiliar hard and chill of the dojo floor –
My first Mu-Shin, no-mindedness.
The group warms up.
Like a child I learn to count again in a new language –
Ichi, Ni, San, Chi, Go, Ryuk, Sich, Huch!
My first exercise in a kind of workout clothes
I've never worn before,
My gi, at first it feels ill fitting –
I move in clumsy, athletic pajamas
With a white belt wrapped around me
I'm not sure that I'm tying the right way.
Almost as soon as I learn the word, "Kata",
Formal exercise, I begin to learn the first one –
Sanchin, from which all Uechi-Ryu,
The dojo's, my family's karate style, flows.
I bow, I rise, hands at my sides,
Raise my arms, focusing, and
Right foot forward, slanted slightly to the left,
I take my first steps towards karate.

Insureomatopeia

II.
MIND

I pivot to the right,
Ninety degrees,
Still in the dojo, yet
Feeling myself surrounded by the openness
Of an empty hand.
In my stance, my upper body tenses,
As a rock on the surface of a frozen pond in March,
Slowly giving way to the season changing's meditative flow.
Hard – Soft – Hard
Arms thrust joyfully in martially artistic expression….
In the middle of Sanchin, I feel as though
I am a living link to the first moments
Master Uechi began to craft and cultivate the first kata.
Embracing the kumite
Between uncertainty and the rest of my mind,
It only adds to me on my karate's lifetime path.
I hear the lazy vibrations of the beetle, and
Smell cherry blossoms wafting towards me on breezes
Rising Heaveneverward to me on top of Yonaha Mountain,
And I feel, for an instant that has stayed with me ever since,
I am Uechi Ryu.

III.
SPIRIT

I slide to the left,
Then turn 180 degrees into the horse stance.
Though it has been checked dozens of times,
I have attempted it so often, I feel
These months have been one long continuous backdrop
Against which I've been practicing
One long, less and less effortful Sanchin.
It is the last class, last night
Of the first year.
I am testing for my green belt, first stripe,
Demonstrating Konchu, the fourth kata, one
I have nowhere near perfected.
Once again, I feel fear. Then,
Unease evaporates into Mu-shin,
Making room for relief, then, joy I must subdue.
As my own father, himself a Yondan – 4th degree blackbelt,
Is testing me tonight.
Before our formal greeting, he says hello –
His hand is friendly, paternal, and warm on my shoulder.
We do concha together, I follow along as best I can, then
He wants to see my Sanchin.
I bow and assume the stance.
He quietly makes a joke, I laugh, and
Sensing me off guard slightly he
Makes my abdomen pay for the lapse
With an expertly pulled riken-uchi –
The Back Fist Strike.

Onomatopoeia

I smile, and the wind knocked out of me
Rises like steam through a green leaf
Descending to steep in a tea boiled
With water drawn from an Okinawan mountain stream.
I have taken the blow,
He smiles.
He holds up his hand, moves from
Where he stood in front of me to beside me.
One moment he is sempei, elder-teacher and
I am kohai, younger-student.
The next, we are demonstrating Sanchin together,
No-mindedly mirror-echoing our movements.
For that minute, we are brothers and fellow-students,
A new pride comes over me and I know a feeling
That, even for all of his wisdom,
Master Kanei Uechi Sr. could never have known –
The joy of a first karate lesson with one's own father.
It is an hour that, until I was living it,
I waited for my whole life to spend with him.
I may take more from martial arts, but
It will never give me anything better.
I bow to the other side of
My first Sanchin's full circle.
It is the class I waited all year to take.

George Jack

Menemsha

Orange communes with infinity here
The sun envelopes the sky like a Chinese lantern
Suspended over gingerbread cottages on Illumination night

The yolk of and egg fluffy enough to have made it into one of
Aalia's perfect breakfast burritos.
Tawny-tinged, untroubled tide and timeless, orbits here.
Cmac discovered the only word that rhymes with orange is
The cockney "Door'inge"

Insureomatopeia

But there is no word to describe
The saffroned-continuum, citrussedly ceilinged, tawny cornea-steeped,
   harmony-lingers
The poor drunk sailors become
The rich drunk sailors become
Guests at the dome-enormous picnic basilica
Where nightly, the owl eyed iris colossus holds court
Sinking into the horizon, peachening Moshups whale blood-red cliffs,
In Chilimark, Ernie Boch's guards briefly taking on the hue
   of Apricotta warriors,
The vast, boundless bisque-mystery,
Tangeine-tinuously margarine melts into the horizon yet again,
Here is where archangel Michaelangelo
Throws his palette to the side and paints this marmaleden hemisphere
This Earth-arched, gentle, Sistene chapel-vastness
With one stroke. The candle dissolves, Entropic of Cancer,
Diminuschendoing softly into this Island-time outworld,
This Vista, Martha's Vineyard.

George Jack

About the Author

George Jack is a multitalented individual. He is a professional voice actor and a poet.

In 2022, George released a humorous holiday- and insurance-themed musical album through the Academy of Insurance with songs such as "O Property O Casualty" and "A Drone Hit a Stranger" which are available on Spotify. His poems from *Indiglorious*, which he reads aloud, can also be found on Spotify.

He is the author of *Popsicle Insurance*, the only book published by the Academy of Insurance specifically for children. George also co-authored of *Don't Play Catch With Jelly*, another delightful children's book.

George grew up in Windham, New Hampshire, and attended Plymouth State University. He currently lives in Concord with his wife and two daughters.

www.ingramcontent.com/pod-product-compliance
Lightning Source LLC
Chambersburg PA
CBHW061741070526
44585CB00024B/2763